# TOTALLY BLACKED OUT™

# ADVENTURE TALES

## BLACKOUT GAMES™

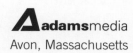

Aadamsmedia
Avon, Massachusetts

Published by
Adams Media, a division of F+W Media, Inc.
57 Littlefield Street, Avon, MA 02322. U.S.A.
www.adamsmedia.com

Totally Blacked Out and Blackout Games are trademarks of
Adams Media, a division of F+W Media, Inc.

ISBN-10: 1-4405-3275-3
ISBN-13: 978-1-4405-3275-7

Printed in the United States of America.

10   9   8   7   6   5   4   3   2   1

This publication is designed to provide accurate and authoritative information
with regard to the subject matter covered. It is sold with the understanding
that the publisher is not engaged in rendering legal, accounting, or other
professional advice. If legal advice or other expert assistance is required, the
services of a competent professional person should be sought.
—From a *Declaration of Principles* jointly adopted by a Committee of the
American Bar Association and a Committee of Publishers and Associations

Many of the designations used by manufacturers and sellers to distinguish
their product are claimed as trademarks. Where those designations appear in
this book and Adams Media was aware of a trademark claim, the designations
have been printed with initial capital letters.

*This book is available at quantity discounts for bulk purchases.*
*For information, please call 1-800-289-0963.*

# CONTENTS

# INTRODUCTION

Finally—a word game that *encourages* you to scribble outside the lines! Combining the simplicity of word search with the creativity of magnetic poetry, *Adventure Tales Blackout Games™* blows those boring, been-there-done-that puzzles out of the water.

Taking gaming to the next level, this book inspires you to think outside the puzzle and look at your favorite (or least favorite) authors' works with a new perspective. Through blacking out words and phrases, you can transform classic pieces of literature into outrageous, poetic, or truly bizarre messages. You'll feel like a kid again as you black out words in the shape of a whale in a passage from *Moby Dick Or, the Whale* or create a fortune cookie message with words plucked ~~struck~~ from *The Legends of King Arthur and His Knights*. With *Adventure Tales Blackout Games™*, you'll absolutely love rewriting the perilous journeys of *Gulliver's Travels into Several Remote Nations of the World*, *Swiss Family Robinson*, and so much more—one blacked-out word at a time!

## HOW TO USE THIS BOOK

Inside this book, you'll find more than 100 puzzles to complete. Each chapter includes detailed directions and a completed example to inspire you. You'll create original messages by blacking out unused words with a marker, but be careful—once they're hidden behind that layer of ink, they're gone forever!

Here's how you get started:

1. Grab a marker or pen; the darker the better.
2. Read the passage carefully and think about what messages can be created out of your favorite words.
3. Make a small mark identifying each word you want to use in your poem (unless you have an awesome memory).
4. ~~Cross~~ black out everything else.
5. When you're done, your message will read like a complete (and perhaps incredibly poetic!) thought.

## NOTE:

To prevent your genius from bleeding through the pages, please place a piece of paper or card stock behind the page before you begin your Totally Blacked Out™ fun.

# CHAPTER ONE

# LITERATURE'S ALPHABET

We're starting with the basics for this first chapter: the alphabet. Sure, it sounds like a breeze, but you've really never seen the alphabet quite like this before. In the following puzzles, you'll have to create a message only using words that begin with the letters assigned to that puzzle, so make sure to pay close attention to your favorite adventure stories. If you get stuck, try starting your message at the bottom of the page or in the middle of the passage like the example we've provided, and remember that you don't always have to use the words in the order that they appear. You may also find it helpful to also search *within* words to help complete your message.

**Create a message using words that begin with the letter "F".**

From Jack London's *Call of the Wild*

**Message:** few faint from fire

1

**Create a message using words that begin with the letters
"A," "B," and "C."**

He had broken into a run now, and as he
advanced he raised his mighty spear, while I
halted and fitting an arrow to my bow took as
steady aim as I could. I was somewhat longer
than usual, for I must confess that the sight
of this awful man had wrought upon my nerves
to such an extent that my knees were anything
but steady. What chance had I against this
mighty warrior for whom even the fiercest
cave bear had no terrors! Could I hope to best
one who slaughtered the sadok and dyryth
single-handed! I shuddered; but, in fairness to
myself, my fear was more for Dian than for my
own fate.

From Edgar Rice Burroughs's *At the Earth's Core*

3

**Create a message using words that begin with vowels.**

Our ~~direct course towards it lay through a~~ ~~rather populous part of the bay; but desirous~~ ~~as we were of evading the natives and securing~~ ~~an unmolested retreat to the mountains, we~~ ~~determined, by taking a circuit through some~~ extensive ~~thickets, to avoid their vicinity~~ ~~altogether. The heavy rain that still conti~~nued ~~to fall without intermission favoured our~~ ~~enterprise, as it drove the~~ islanders ~~into their~~ ~~houses and prevented any casual meeting with~~ ~~them. Our heavy frocks soon became completely~~ ~~saturated with water, and by their weight and~~ ~~that of the~~ articles ~~we had concealed beneath~~ ~~them, not a little impeded our progress. But~~ ~~it was no time to pause when at any moment we~~ ~~might be surprised by a body of the savages and~~ ~~forced at the very outset to relinquish our~~ ~~undertaking.~~

From Herman Melville's *Typee, a Romance of the South Seas*

5

**Create a message using words that begin with the letters "C," "D," "E," and "F."**

~~It became~~ clear ~~to me that whatever danger threatened an occupant of the room could not come either from the window or the door. My attention was speedily drawn, as I have already remarked to you, to this ventilator, and to the bell rope which hung down to the bed. The discovery that this was a dummy, and that the bed was clamped to the floor, instantly gave rise to the suspicion that the rope was there as bridge for something passing through the hole, and coming to the bed. The idea of a snake instantly occurred to me, and when I coupled it with my knowledge that the doctor was furnished with a supply of creatures from India, I felt that I was probably on the right track.~~

From Sir Arthur Conan Doyle's *Adventures of Sherlock Holmes*

**Create a message using words that begin with consonants.**

A second storm came ~~upon us~~, which carried ~~us away with~~ the same ~~impetuosity~~ westward, ~~and~~ drove ~~us~~ so ~~out of~~ the way ~~of all~~ human commerce, that, had ~~all our~~ lives been saved ~~as~~ ~~to the sea, we were rather in danger of being devoured by savages than ever returning to our own country. In this distress, the wind still blowing very hard, one of our men early in the morning cried out, "Land!" and we had no sooner run out of the cabin to look out,~~ in ~~hopes of~~ seeing whereabouts in the ~~world we were, than the ship struck upon a sand,~~ and in a ~~moment, her~~ motion being so stopped, ~~the sea broke over her in such a manner, that we expected we should all have~~ perished ~~immediately.~~

From Daniel Defoe's *The Life and Adventures of Robinson Crusoe*

**Create a message using words that begin with the letters
"F," "G," "H," and "I."**

As I was entertaining the court with these kind
of feats, there arrived an express to inform his
Majesty, that some of his subjects, riding near
the place where I was first taken up, had seen
a great black substance lying on the ground,
very oddly shaped, extended its edges round as
wide as his Majesty's bed-chamber, and rising
up in the middle as high as a man; that it was no
living creature, as they at first apprehended,
for it lay on the grass without motion; and some
of them had walked round it several times: that,
by mounting upon each other's shoulders, they
had got to the top, which was flat and even, and,
stamping upon it, they found that it was hollow
within; that they humbly conceived it might be
something belonging to the Man-Mountain.

From Jonathan Swift's *Gulliver's Travels into
Several Remote Nations of the World*

**Create a message using words that begin with vowels.**

Suddenly out of the darkness, out of the night, there swooped something with a swish like an aeroplane. The whole group of us were covered for an instant by a canopy of leathery wings, and I had a momentary vision of a long, snake-like neck, a fierce, red, greedy eye, and a great snapping beak, filled, to my amazement, with little, gleaming teeth. The next instant it was gone—and so was our dinner. A huge black shadow, twenty feet across, skimmed up into the air; for an instant the monster wings blotted out the stars, and then it vanished over the brow of the cliff above us. We all sat in amazed silence round the fire, like the heroes of Virgil when the Harpies came down upon them.

From Sir Arthur Conan Doyle's *The Lost World*

**Create a message using words that begin with consonants.**

The sea-reach of the Thames stretched before us like the beginning of an interminable waterway. In the offing the sea and the sky were welded together without a joint, and in the luminous space the tanned sails of the barges drifting up with the tide seemed to stand still in red clusters of canvas sharply peaked, with gleams of varnished spirits. A haze rested on the low shores that ran out to sea in vanishing flatness. The air was dark above Gravesend, and farther back still seemed condensed into a mournful gloom, brooding motionless over the biggest, and the greatest, town on earth. The Director of Companies was our captain and our host. We four affectionately watched his back as he stood in the bows looking to seaward. On the whole river there was nothing that looked half so nautical.

From Joseph Conrad's *Heart of Darkness*

**Create a message using words that begin with consonants.**

Beowulf donned then his battle-equipments,

Cared little for life; inlaid and most ample,

The hand-woven corslet which could cover his
    body,

Must the wave-deeps explore, that war might be
    powerless

To harm the great hero, and the hating one's
    grasp might

Not peril his safety; his head was protected

By the light-flashing helmet that should mix
    with the bottoms,

Trying the eddies, treasure-emblazoned,

Encircled with jewels, as in seasons long past

The weapon-smith worked it, wondrously made it,

With swine-bodies fashioned it, that
    thenceforward no longer

Brand might bite it, and battle-sword hurt it.

And that was not least of helpers in prowess

He has Unferth's sword in his hand.

That Hrothgar's spokesman had lent him when
    straitened.

From Alfred John Wyatt's *Beowulf*

17

# CHAPTER TWO

# FEW AND FAR BETWEEN

Let's find out how much you really love the stories you've heard since you were little. To solve the puzzles in this chapter, you'll need to black out the least amount of words possible. With several world-renown passages in front of you, it may not seem like a hard task to create your very own poem, but the difficulty here lies in creating an *original* message that sounds more like you than straight from the pages of these beloved stories. Once you're feeling a little creative, take a look at the example we've done and get ready to pen your very own classic tale.

Dorothy leaned ▮▮▮▮▮ upon her hand and gazed ▮▮▮ at ▮ Scarecrow. ▮▮▮▮▮ stuffed ▮▮▮▮▮ eyes, nose ▮ mouth painted on ▮▮▮▮▮ ▮▮▮▮ some Munchkin ▮▮ perched on this head, and ▮▮▮▮▮▮ a blue suit ▮▮▮▮ worn and faded, ▮▮ had also been stuffed with straw. On the feet were some old boots with blue tops, such as every man wore ▮▮▮▮▮ and the figure was raised above the stalks of corn by means of the pole stuck up its back.

From L. Frank Baum's *The Wonderful Wizard of Oz*

**Message:** Dorothy leaned upon her hand and gazed at Scarecrow./ stuffed eyes, nose mouth painted on/ some Munchkin perched on this head, and a blue suit worn and faded, had also been stuffed with straw./ On the feet were some old boots with blue tops, such as every man wore and the figure was raised above the stalks of corn by means of the pole stuck up its back.

The deck was deserted, and he crawled to the extreme end of it, near the flag-pole. There he doubled up in limp agony, for the Wheeling "stogie" joined with the surge and jar of the screw to sieve out his soul. His head swelled; sparks of fire danced before his eyes; his body seemed to lose weight, while his heels wavered in the breeze. He was fainting from seasickness, and a roll of the ship tilted him over the rail on to the smooth lip of the turtle-back. Then a low, gray mother-wave swung out of the fog, tucked Harvey under one arm, so to speak, and pulled him off and away to leeward ; the great green closed over him, and he went quietly to sleep.

From Rudyard Kipling's *Captains Courageous*

When the sun had set, and darkness came on, then they slept near the hawsers of their ships. But when the mother of dawn, rosy-fingered morning, appeared, straightway then they set sail for the spacious camp of the Achæans, and to them far-darting Apollo sent a favourable gale. But they erected the mast and expanded the white sails. The wind streamed into the bosom of the sail; and as the vessel briskly ran, the dark wave roared loudly around the keel; but she scudded through the wave, holding on her way. But when they reached the wide armament of the Greeks, they drew up the black ship on the continent, far upon the sand, and stretched long props under it; but they dispersed themselves through their tents and ships.

From Homer's *The Iliad*

The fisherman came a step nearer, and addressed himself to me. "Mr. Betteredge," he said, "I have a word to say to you about the young woman's death. Four foot out, broadwise, along the side of the Spit, there's a shelf of rock, about half fathom down under the sand. My question is—why didn't she strike that? If she slipped, by accident, from off the Spit, she fell in where there's foothold at the bottom, at a depth that would barely cover her to the waist. She must have waded out, or jumped out, into the Deeps beyond—or she wouldn't be missing now. No accident, sir! The Deeps of the Quicksand have got her. And they have got her by her own act." After that testimony from a man whose knowledge was to be relied on, the Sergeant was silent.

From Wilkie Collins's *The Moonstone*

The lieutenant of the youth's company had encountered a soldier who had fled screaming at the first volley of his comrades. Behind the lines these two were acting a little isolated scene. The man was, blubbering and staring with sheep-like eyes at the lieutenant, who had seized him by the collar and was pommeling him. He drove him back into the ranks with many blows. The soldier went mechanically, dully, with his animal-like eyes upon the officer. Perhaps there was to him a divinity expressed in the voice of the other—stern, hard, with no reflection of fear in it. He tried to reload his gun, but his shaking hands prevented. The lieutenant was obliged to assist him. The men dropped here and there like bundles.

From Stephen Crane's *The Red Badge of Courage*

By-and-by the Warner lightship, afar out at sea beyond Spithead, and the Nab light beyond her again, could be seen twinkling in the distance, while the moon presently rose in the eastern sky right over Fort Cumberland; and then, all at once, there was a sudden flash, which, coming right in front of me, dazzled my eyes like lightning. This was followed by a single but very startling "Bang!" that thundered out from the flagship, which, swinging round with the outgoing ebb tide, was now lying almost athwart stream, with her high, square stern gallery overhanging the sloping shore below the hotel, looking as if the old craft had taken the ground and fired the gun that had startled us as a signal of distress—so, at least, with the vivid imagination of boyhood, thought I!

From John Hutcheson's *Crown and Anchor*

Alice lifted up her head in some alarm. There was no one to be seen, and her first thought was that she must have been dreaming about the Lion and the Unicorn and those queer Anglo-Saxon Messengers. However, there was the great dish still lying at her feet, on which she had tried to cut the plum-cake, "So I wasn't dreaming, after all," she said to herself, "unless—unless we're all part of the same dream. Only I do hope it's MY dream, and not the Red King's! I don't like belonging to another person's dream," she went on in a rather complaining tone: "I've a great mind to go and wake him, and see what happens!"

From Lewis Carroll's *Through the Looking Glass*

It was about five months after this return home, that her friends were alarmed by her sudden disappearance for the second time. Three days elapsed, and nothing was heard of her. On the fourth her corpse was found floating in the Seine,* near the shore which is opposite the Quartier of the Rue Saint Andree, and at a point not very far distant from the secluded neighborhood of the Barriere du Roule. The atrocity of this murder, (for it was at once evident that murder had been committed,) the youth and beauty of the victim, and, above all, her previous notoriety, conspired to produce intense excitement in the minds of the sensitive Parisians. I can call to mind no similar occurrence producing so general and so intense an effect.

From Edgar Allan Poe's "The Mystery of Marie Roget"

Confused by the motion and a blinding sleet-shower that had come on, and forgetting the tremendous strain on the cable, I cast the slack off the bitts and left it loose. There was then only one turn of the chain round the drum, enough in ordinary weather to prevent it running out. But now my first heave on the winch-lever started it slipping, and in an instant it was whizzing out of the hawse-pipe and overboard. I tried to stop it with my foot, stumbled at a heavy plunge of the yacht, heard something snap below, and saw the last of it disappear. The yacht fell off the wind and drifted astern. I shouted, and had the sense to hoist the reefed foresail at once. Davies had her in hand in no time, and was steering south-west.

From Erskine Childers's *The Riddle of the Sands*

# CHAPTER THREE

# *THE GREATEST EXPECTATION*

Time for a ~~little~~ lot of fun! In this chapter, we're giving you full permission to wreak havoc on all your favorite (or most loathed) stories. That's right, in order to finish the following puzzles, you'll need to create a message by blacking out as many words as possible. Just remember that you should still be left with a complete thought at the end of each ink-filled puzzle. If you're looking for more of a challenge, try to beat our sample puzzle or test your blackout skills against your friends.

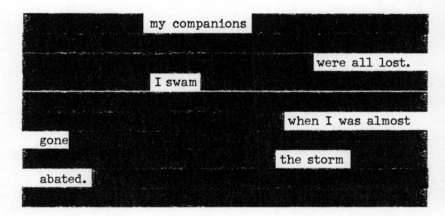

From Jonathan Swift's *Gulliver's Travels into
Several Remote Nations of the World*

**Message:** my companions were all lost./ I swam when I was almost gone/ the storm abated.

Once, when a strong body of the continental army held the Four Comers for a whole summer, orders had been received from Washington himself, never to leave the door of Harvey Birch unwatched. The command was rigidly obeyed, and during this long period the pedler was unseen; the detachment was withdrawn, and the following night Birch re-entered his dwelling. The father of Harvey had been greatly molested, in consequence of the suspicious character of the son. But, notwithstanding the most minute scrutiny into the conduct of the old man, no fact could be substantiated against him to his injury, and his property was too small to keep alive the zeal of patriots by profession. Its confiscation and purchase would not have rewarded their trouble. Age and sorrow were now about to spare him further molestation, for the lamp of life had been drained of its oil.

From James Fenimore Cooper's *The Spy: A Tale of the Neutral Ground*

He was close to the edge of a steep-walled basin; and leading to it was a narrow, steep gully, down which the beaten trail went. Riding closer he saw that two poles were set close to the wall of the gully, and from one of them dangled a short, frayed hempen rope. There was a water hole in the basin, surrounded by a muddy flat, and everywhere were the tracks of cattle. As he hesitated to decide whether or not it would be worth while to ride through the depression he chanced to look south, and the question decided itself. Spurring savagely, he leaned forward in the saddle, the wind playing a stem song in his ears, a call to battle for his ranch, his pride, and his hatred for foul work.

From Clarence Mulford's *Hopalong Cassidy*

Cal. Art thou afeard?

Steph. No, monster, not I.

Cal. Be not afeard; the isle is full of noises,

Sounds and sweet airs, that give delight and
    hurt not.

Sometimes a thousand twangling instruments

Will hum about mine ears; and sometime voices.

That, if I then had waked after long sleep.

Will make me sleep again : and then, in dreaming,

The clouds methought would open and show riches

Ready to drop upon me, that, when I waked,

I cried to dream again.

Steph. This will prove a brave kingdom to me,
    where I

shall have my music for nothing.

Cal. When Prospero is destroyed.

Steph. That shall be by and by:

I remember the story

Trin. The sound is going away;

let's follow it, and after do our work.

Steph. Lead, monster;

we'll follow. I would I could see this taborer;

he lays it on.

Trin, Wilt come? I'll follow, Stephano.

From William Shakespeare's *The Tempest*

Two years ago, after the shooting of le Blois, by some hitch in their almost perfect arrangements, one of the four was recognized by a detective as having been seen leaving le Blois's house on the Avenue Kleber, and he was shadowed for three days, in the hope that the four might be captured together, In the end he discovered he was being watched, and made a bolt for liberty. He was driven to bay in a cafe in Bordeaux—they had followed him from Paris; and before he was killed he shot a sergeant de ville and two other policemen. He was photographed, and the print was circulated throughout Europe, but who he was or what he was, even what nationality he was, is a mystery to this day.

From Edgar Wallace's *The Four Just Men*

The room used as a study was on the ground floor, and had windows on the west and on the south. Those on the west (French windows) opened on a loggia; those on the south opened right into the dense tangle of a neglected shrubbery. The place possessed an oppressive atmosphere of loneliness, for which in some measure its history may have been responsible. The silence, seemingly intensified by each whisper that sped through the elms and crept about the shrubbery, grew to such a stillness that I told myself I had experienced nothing like it since crossing with a caravan I had slept in the desert. Yet noisy, whirling London was within gunshot of us; and this, though hard enough to believe, was a reflection oddly comforting. Only one train of thought was possible, and this I pursued at random.

From Sax Rohmer's *The Quest of the Sacred Slipper*

This road brought him presently into a field of ruins, in the midst of which, in the side of a hill, he saw an open door and (not far off) a single stunted pine no greater than a currant-bush. The place was desert and very secret: a voice spoke in the count's bosom that there was something here to his advantage. He tied his horse to the pine-tree, took his flint and steel in his hand to make a light, and entered into the hill. The doorway opened on a passage of old Roman masonry, which shortly after branched in two. The count took the turning to the right, and followed it, groping forward in the dark, till he was brought up by a kind of fence, about elbow-high, which extended quite across the passage.

From Robert Louis Stevenson's *The Master of Ballantrae: A Winter's Tale*

In the afternoon we cleared the column and had an open road for some hours. The land now had a tilt eastward, as if we were moving towards the valley of a great river. Soon we began to meet little parties of men coming from the east with a new look in their faces. The first lots of wounded had been the ordinary thing you see on every front, and there had been some pretence at organization. But these new lots were very weary and broken; they were often barefoot, and they seemed to have lost their transport and to be starving. You would find a group stretched by the roadside in the last stages of exhaustion. Then would come a party limping along, so tired that they never turned their heads to look at us.

From John Buchan's *Greenmantle*

I touched a rotting wooden post and slimy timbers. I had reached one bound of my watery prison. More fire fell from above, and the scream of hysteria quivered, unuttered, in my throat. Keeping myself afloat with increasing difficulty in my heavy garments, I threw my head back and raised my eyes. No more drops fell, and no more drops would fall; but it was merely a question of time for the floor to collapse. For it was beginning to a emit a dull, red glow. The room above me was in flames! It was drops of burning oil from the lamp, finding passage through the cracks in the crazy flooring, which had fallen about me—for the death trap had reclosed, I suppose, mechanically.

From Sax Rohmer's *The Insidious Dr. Fu-Manchu*

"Whenever my uncle visited us," said the Prince, "or when my late father went to see him, the journey was always made by sea: and in order to do this it was necessary to go in a very roundabout way between Itoby and Yan. Now, I shall do nothing of this kind. It is beneath the dignity of a prince to go out of his way on account of capes, peninsulas, and promontories. I shall march from my palace to that of my uncle in a straight line, I shall go across the country, and no obstacle shall cause me to deviate from my course. Mountains and hills shall be tunnelled, rivers shall be bridged, houses shall be levelled, a road shall be cut through forests, and when I have finished my march, the course over which I have passed shall be a mathematically straight line."

From Frank Stockton's "Prince Hassak's March"

# CHAPTER FOUR

# A DIFFERENT POINT OF VIEW

We're turning everything upside down in this chapter. Just like before, you'll need to black out words to create a message, but this time, you'll need to construct a sentence that can be read from the bottom to the top of the page. Still can't wrap your head around this new outlook? Use our blackout example for ideas on how to start creating your message. You're sure to have a great time starting at the bottom with these topsy-turvy puzzles!

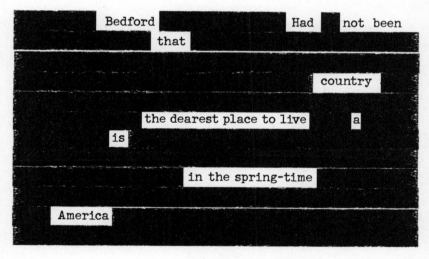

From Herman Melville's *Moby-Dick Or, the Whale*

**Message:** America in the spring-time is the dearest place to live/ a country that Bedford Had not been

I think I have never experienced an identical sensation in my life; my tongue clave to the roof of my mouth; my heart suspended its functions; and I felt my eyes start forward in their sockets. I had not thought my constitution capable of such profound and helpless fear, nor had I hitherto paid proper respect to the memory of Charles I. I would gladly have closed my eyes in order that I might not witness the downward sweep of the fatal blade, but the lids seemed to be paralyzed. Never whilst memory serves me can I forget one detail of the appearance of that frightful old devil; and never can I forget my gratitude to that unseen captor, the man who had seized me from behind, and who now, alone, averted the blade from my neck.

From Sax Rohmer's *Tales of Secret Egypt*

All at once, at the moment when the executioner's assistants were preparing to obey the phlegmatic order of Charmolue, he strode across the balustrade of the gallery, seized the rope with feet, knees, and hands, glided down the facade like a drop of rain down a pane of glass; ran up to the two men with the swiftness of a cat that has fallen from a roof; felled both of them to the ground with his enormous fists; bore off the Egyptian on one arm, as a girl would her doll, and at one bound he was in the church, holding up the young girl above his head and shouting with terrific voice "Sanctuary! Sanctuary!" This was all done with the rapidity of lightning.

From Victor Hugo's *The Hunchback of Notre-Dame*

"That's him," replied Mr. Murch. "Lodged in the bone at the back of the skull... These bright scratches you see were made by the doctor's instruments. These other marks were made by the rifling of the barrel a barrel like this one." He tapped the revolver. "Same make, same calibre. There is no other that marks the bullet just like this." With the pistol in its case between them, Trent and the inspector looked into each other's eyes for some moments. Trent was the first to speak. "This mystery is all wrong," he observed. "It is insanity. The symptoms of mania are very marked. Let us see how we stand. We were not in any doubt, I believe, about Manderson having dispatched Marlowe in the car to Southampton, or about Marlowe having gone, returning late last night, many hours after the murder was committed."

From E.C. Bentley's *Trent's Last Case*

The sleepy village of Gavrillac, a half-league removed from the main road to Rennes, and therefore undisturbed by the world's traffic, lay in a curve of the River Meu, at the foot, and straggling halfway up the slope, of the shallow hill that was crowned by the squat manor. By the time Gavrillac had paid tribute to its seigneur partly in money and partly in service tithes to the Church, and imposts to the King, it was hard put to it to keep body and soul together with what remained. Yet, hard as conditions were in Gavrillac, they were not so hard as in many other parts of France, not half so hard, for instance, as with the wretched feudatories of the great Lord of La Tour d'Azyr.

From Rafael Sabatini's *Scaramouche: A Romance of the French Revolution*

There was no suggestion of form in the utter blackness; only could be seen a pair of eyes gleaming like live coals. Henry indicated with his head a second pair, and a third. A circle of the gleaming eyes had drawn about their camp. Now and again a pair of eyes moved, or disappeared to appear again a moment later. The unrest of the dogs had been increasing, and they stampeded, in a surge of sudden fear, to the near side of the fire, cringing and crawling about the legs of the men. . . . The commotion caused the circle of eyes to shift restlessly for a moment and even to withdraw a bit, but it settled down again as the dogs became quiet.

From Jack London's *White Fang*

The path upon which the party travelled was now so narrow as not to admit, with any sort of convenience, above two riders abreast, and began to descend into a dingle, traversed by a brook whose banks were broken, swampy, and overgrown with dwarf willows. Cedric and Athelstane, who were at the head of their retinue, saw the risk of being attacked at this pass; but neither of them having had much practice in war, no better mode of preventing the danger occurred to them than that they should hasten through the defile as fast as possible. Advancing, therefore, without much order, they had just crossed the brook with a part of their followers, when they were assailed in front, flank, and rear at once.

From Sir Walter Scott's *Ivanhoe*

We made good time; and a couple of hours before sunset we stood upon the high confines of the Valley of Holiness, and our eyes swept it from end to end and noted its features. That is, its large features. These were the three masses of buildings. They were distant and isolated temporalities shrunken to toy constructions in the lonely waste of what seemed a desert—and was. Such a scene is always mournful, it is so impressively still, and looks so steeped in death. But there was a sound here which interrupted the stillness only to add to its mournfulness; this was the faint far sound of tolling bells which floated fitfully to us on the passing breeze, and go faintly, so softly, that we hardly knew whether we heard it with our ears or with our spirits.

From Mark Twain's *A Connecticut Yankee in King Arthur's Court*

All the afternoon and evening the boys continued to let down and draw up their net, sometimes bringing in only a few tiny fish, sometimes getting half a dozen of the larger kind. By nightfall they had satisfied the cravings of hunger, and felt stronger and better. One or two sails had been seen during the day, but always at such distances that it was evident at once that they could not pass within hail. That night, fatigued with their exertions, both laid down and went to sleep until morning, and slept more comfortably than before; for they had fastened a piece of the sail tightly on the top of the raft, and lay softly suspended in that, instead of being balanced upon a narrow and uncomfortable plank.

From G.A. Henty's *The Young Buglers: A Tale of the Peninsular War*

He was glad when he had passed the spot, and again that night, as he looked back, he saw the strange effect of light and darkness which produced the impression of someone standing in the shadow of the last buttress space. The illusion was so perfect that he thought he could make out the figure of a man, in a long loose cape that napped in the wind. He had passed the wrought-iron gates now—he was in the churchyard, and it was then that he first became aware of a soft, low, droning, sound which seemed to fill the air all about him. He stopped for a moment to listen; what was it? Where was the noise? It grew more distinct as he passed along the flagged stone path which led to the north door. Yes, it certainly came from inside the church.

From John Meade Falkner's *The Nebuly Coat*

# CHAPTER FIVE

# SWITCHING PERSPECTIVE

Think you've mastered flipping around messages? Think again. Like the previous chapter, you'll need to visualize the passages a little differently to solve the following puzzles. However, instead of creating a sentence that can be read from the bottom to the top of the page, this time you'll have to make it read from right to left. Not sure where to start? Glance at our sample for inspiration.

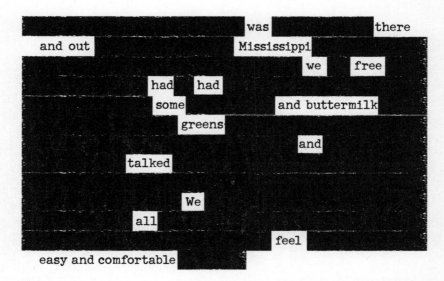

From Mark Twain's *The Adventures of Huckleberry Finn*

**Message:** there was Mississippi/ out and free we had had buttermilk and some greens and talked/ we all feel comfortable and easy

The woods across the line were but the scarred and blackened ruins of woods; for the most part the trees had fallen, but a certain proportion still stood, dismal gray stems, with dark-brown foliage instead of green. On our side the fire had done no more than scorch the nearer trees; it had failed to secure its footing. In one place the woodmen had been at work on Saturday; trees, felled and freshly trimmed, lay in a clearing, with heaps of sawdust, by the sawing machine and its engine. Hard by was a temporary hut, deserted. There was not a breath of wind this morning, and everything was strangely still. Even the birds were hushed, and as we hurried along, I and the artilleryman talked in whispers, and looked now and again over our shoulders. Once or twice we stopped to listen.

From H.G. Wells's *The War of the Worlds*

Driving the spurs into our horses, we rushed at a gallop round the house, and in a moment we were among the ruffians. Sapt told me afterward that he killed a man, and I believe him; but I saw no more of him. With a cut I split the head of a fellow on a brown horse, and he fell to the ground. Then I found myself opposite a big man, and I was half conscious of another to my right. It was too warm to stay, and with a simultaneous action I drove my spurs into my horse again and my sword full into the big man's breast. His bullet whizzed past my ear—I could almost swear it touched it. I wrenched at the sword, but it would not come, and I dropped it and galloped after Sapt, whom I now saw about twenty yards ahead.

From Anthony Hope's *The Prisoner of Zenda*

Soon after seven o'clock that evening the storm which had threatened all day burst in its full fury. A raging gale tore at the dilapidated roofs of this squalid corner of the great city, and lashed the mud of the streets into miniature cascades. Soon the rain fell in torrents; one clap of thunder followed on another with appalling rapidity, and the dull, leaden sky was rent with vivid flashes of lightning. Chauvelin, who had paid his daily visit to the Captain in charge of the prisoner in the Rue de la Planchette, was unable to proceed homewards. For the moment the street appeared impassable. Wrapped in his cloak, he decided to wait in the disused storage-room below until it became possible for an unfortunate pedestrian to sally forth into the open.

From Baroness Emmuska Orczy's *The Triumph of the Scarlet Pimpernel*

On the sea, upon the furthest limits of vision, appeared an advancing streak of seething foam, resembling a narrow white ribbon, drawn rapidly along the level surface of the water by its two ends, which were lost in the darkness. It rushed the brig, passed under, stretching out on each side; and on each side the water became noisy, breaking into numerous and tiny wavelets, a mimicry of an immense agitation. Yet the vessel in the midst of this sudden and loud disturbance remained as motionless and steady as if she had been securely moored between the stone walls of a safe dock. In a few moments the line of foam and ripple running swiftly north passed at once beyond sight and earshot, leaving no trace on the unconquerable calm. "Now this is very curious," began Shaw.

From Joseph Conrad's *The Rescue: A Romance of the Shallows*

We must now go on board, and our first cause of surprise will be the deception relative to the tonnage of the schooner, when viewed from a distance. Instead of a small vessel of about ninety tons, we discover that she is upwards of two hundred; that her breadth of beam is enormous; and that those spars which appeared so light and elegant, are of unexpected dimensions. Her decks are of narrow fir planks, without the least spring or rise; her ropes are of Manilla hemp, neatly secured to copper belaying-pins, and coiled down on the deck, whose whiteness is well contrasted with the bright green paint of her bulwarks; her capstern and binnacles are cased in fluted mahogany, and ornamented with brass.

From Frederick Marryat's *The Pirate, and the Three Cutters*

The vessel had recently passed a lot of wreckage, that betokened they were not far from the spot where some ship, less lucky than themselves, had been overwhelmed by the treacherous waters of the ill-fated bay; and the news that a waif was now in sight, supporting a stray survivor, affected all hearts on board, and roused their sympathies at once. The captain of the New England barque had already adjusted the telescope, that he carried in true sailor fashion tucked under his left arm, to his "weather-eye," and was looking eagerly in the direction pointed out by the seaman, before he received the answer from aloft to his second hail. But he could not as yet see what the lookout had discovered, from the fact of the waves being still high and his place of outlook from the deck lower than the other's.

From John Hutcheson's *Picked Up at Sea*

About six miles above the mouth of the Yellowstone, the voyagers landed at Fort Union, the distributing post of the American Fur Company in the western country. It was a stockaded fortress, about two hundred and twenty feet square, pleasantly situated on a high bank. Here they were hospitably entertained by Mr. M'Kenzie, the superintendent, and remained with him three days, enjoying the unusual luxuries of bread, butter, milk, and cheese, for the fort was well supplied with domestic cattle, though it had no garden. The atmosphere of these elevated regions is said to be too dry for the culture of vegetables; yet the voyagers, in coming down the Yellowstone, had met with plums, grapes, cherries, and currants, and had observed ash and elm trees. Where these grow, the climate cannot be incompatible with gardening.

From Washington Irving's *The Adventures of Captain Bonneville*

The bishop did know. Never before in all his wilderness work had he faced such a thing. He knew that Trampas was an evil in the country, and that the Virginian was a good. He knew that the cattle thieves—the rustlers—were gaining in numbers and audacity; that they led many weak young fellows to ruin; that they elected their men to office, and controlled juries; that they were a staring menace to Wyoming. His heart was with the Virginian. But there was his Gospel, that he preached, and believed, and tried to live. He stood looking at the ground and drawing a finger along his eyebrow. He wished that he might have heard nothing about all this.

From Owen Wister's *The Virginian; A Horseman of the Plains*

The volcano had awoke, and the vapour had penetrated the mineral layer heaped up at the bottom of the crater. But would the subterranean fires provoke any violent eruption? This was an event which could not be foreseen. However, even while admitting the possibility of an eruption, it was not probable that the whole of Lincoln Island would suffer from it. The flow of volcanic matter is not always disastrous, and the island had already undergone this trial, as was shown by the streams of lava hardened on the northern slopes of the mountain. Besides, from the shape of the crater—the opening broken in the upper edge—the matter would be thrown to the side opposite the fertile regions of the island. However, the past did not necessarily answer for the future.

From Jules Verne's *The Mysterious Island*

# CHAPTER SIX

# A CLASSIC Q & A

In this chapter, you'll have to answer the fun (and often ridiculous) questions we've provided. Finding an answer in the puzzle may be a little tricky, so feel free to use a little imagination and a lot of creativity to uncover the possibilities for responses. As you can see from our blackout example, your message may not be 100 percent truthful when all is said and done, but it's guaranteed to be absolutely hilarious! Now, the real question is: Are you ready for this challenge?

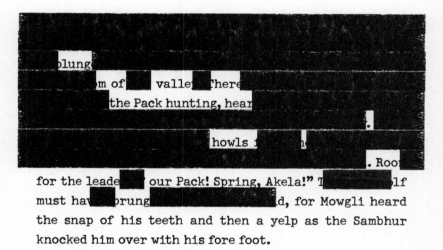

plung

m of    valle There

the Pack hunting, hear

howls

. Roo

for the leade    our Pack! Spring, Akela!" T        lf
must hav   prung        d, for Mowgli heard
the snap of his teeth and then a yelp as the Sambhur
knocked him over with his fore foot.

From Rudyard Kipling's *The Jungle Book*

**Message:** yell and snort the wicked, bitter howls. Spring!/ hear the snap of teeth and then a yelp as ur knocked over

**What would you do if you were stuck in the jungle?**

The lioness was now back in the path where she could see the author of the indignity which had been placed upon her. Screaming with rage she suddenly charged, leaping high into the air toward Tarzan, but when her huge body struck the limb on which Tarzan had been, Tarzan was no longer there. Instead he perched lightly upon a smaller branch twenty feet above the raging captive. For a moment Sabor hung half across the branch, while Tarzan mocked, and hurled twigs and branches at her unprotected face. Presently the beast dropped to the earth again and Tarzan came quickly to seize the rope, but Sabor, had now found that it was only a slender cord that held her, and grasping it in her huge jaws -severed it before Tarzan could tighten the strangling noose a second time.

From Edgar Rice Burroughs's *Tarzan of the Apes*

**What would you do if you found a magic lamp?**

He did not omit the least circumstance of
what he saw in crossing the three halls and
the garden, and his taking the lamp, which
he pulled out of his bosom and showed to his
mother : as well as the transparent fruit of
different colours, which he had gathered in
the garden as he returned. But, though these
fruits were precious stones, brilliant as the
sun, she was as ignorant of their worth as her
son. She had been bred in a low rank of life,
and her husband's poverty prevented his being
possessed of jewels, nor had she, her relations,
or neighbours ever seen any; so that we must
not wonder that she regarded them as things of
no value.

From Kate Douglas Wiggin and Nora Smith's
"The Story of Aladdin; or, the Wonderful Lamp"

**Describe your favorite childhood adventure.**

The other pirates were looking their last, too; and they all looked so long that they came near letting the current drift them out of the range of the island. But they discovered the danger in time, and made shift to avert it. About two o'clock in the morning the raft grounded on the bar two hundred yards above the head of the island, and they waded back and forth until they had landed their freight. Part of the little raft's belongings consisted of an old sail, and this they spread over a nook in the bushes for a tent to shelter their provisions; but they themselves would sleep in the open air in good weather, as became outlaws.

From Mark Twain's *The Adventures of Tom Sawyer*

**If you were an animal, what kind would you be?**

The circle had tightened till he could feel the breaths of the huskies on his flanks. He could see them, beyond Spitz and to either side, half crouching for the spring, their eyes fixed upon him. A pause seemed to fall. Every animal was motionless as though turned to stone. Only Spitz quivered and bristled as he staggered back and forth, snarling with horrible menace, as though to frighten off impending death. Then Buck sprang in and out; but while he was in, shoulder had at last squarely met shoulder. The dark circle became a dot on the moon-flooded snow as Spitz disappeared from view. Buck stood and looked on, the successful champion, the dominant primordial beast who had made his kill and found it good.

From Jack London's *Call of the Wild*

**If you were to go on an adventure today, which of your friends would you take and why?**

Immediately, without any order being given, or his place of destination indicated, the coachman set off at a rapid pace, and plunged into the streets of the town. So strange a reception naturally gave milady ample matter for reflection. So; seeing that the young officer did not seem at all disposed for conversation, she reclined in her corner of the carriage, and, one after the other, passed in review all the suppositions which presented themselves to her mind. At the end of a quarter of an hour, however, surprised at the length of the journey, she leant forward toward the window to see whither she was being conducted. Houses were no longer to be seen; trees appeared in the darkness like great black phantoms running after one another. Milady shuddered with apprehension.

From Alexandre Dumas's *The Three Musketeers*

**What would you do if you were stuck on a deserted island with your family?**

For many days we had been tempest-tossed. Six times had the darkness closed over a wild and terrific scene, and returning light as often brought but renewed distress, for the raging storm increased in fury until on the seventh day all hope was lost. We were driven completely out of our course; no conjecture could be formed as to our whereabouts. The crew had lost heart, and were utterly exhausted by incessant labour. The riven masts had gone by the board, leaks had been sprung in every direction, and the water, which rushed in, gained upon us rapidly. Instead of reckless oaths, the seamen now uttered frantic cries to God for mercy, mingled with strange and often ludicrous vows, to be performed should deliverance be granted.

From Johann David Wyss's *The Swiss Family Robinson*

**Describe your last adventure.**

But while we were enjoying ourselves in eating and drinking, and recovering ourselves from the fatigue of the sea, the island on a sudden trembled, and shook us terribly. The motion was perceived on board the ship, and we were called upon to re-embark speedily, or we should all be lost; for what we took for an island proved to be the back of a sea monster. The nimblest got into the sloop, others betook themselves to swimming; but for myself, I was still upon the back of the creature when he dived into the sea, and I had time only to catch hold of a piece of wood that we had brought out of the ship.

From Kate Douglas Wiggin and Nora Smith's
"The Story of Sinbad the Voyager"

**What's the worst trip you've ever been on?**

On the eleventh day we sighted Cape Portland, over which towered Mount Myrdals Yokul, which, the weather being clear, we made out very readily. The cape itself is nothing but a huge mount of granite standing naked and alone to meet the Atlantic waves. The Valkyrie kept off the coast, steering to the westward. On all sides were to be seen whole "schools" of whales and sharks. After some hours we came in sight of a solitary rock in the ocean, forming a mighty vault, through which the foaming waves poured with intense fury. The islets of Westman appeared to leap from the ocean, being so low in the water as scarcely to be seen until you were right upon them. From that moment the schooner was steered to the westward in order to round Cape Reykjanes, the western point of Iceland.

From Jules Verne's *A Journey to the Centre of the Earth*

# A LITTLE FAUX WISDOM

What's the best part of getting Chinese takeout? The fortune cookie, of course! In this chapter, you'll get to try your hand at creating some of your very own, so get ready to summon your inner Confucius. You'll have to use the words in following passages to form a profound statement worthy of a cookie. If you're having trouble coming up with some sage advice, look to our blackout example for guidance.

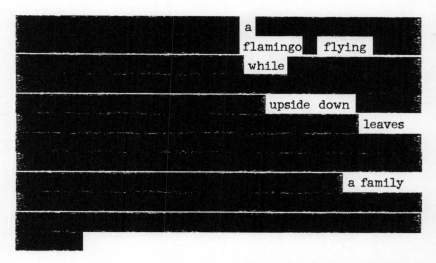

From J.M. Barrie's *Peter and Wendy*

**Message:** a flamingo flying while upside down leaves a family

About a hundred paces from the spot where the two friends were, with their looks fixed on the distance, and their ears attentive, whilst they imbibed the sparkling wine of La Malgue, behind a bare, and torn, and weather-worn wall, was the small village of the Catalans. One day a mysterious colony quitted Spain and settled on the tongue of land on which it is to this day. It arrived from no one knew where, and spoke an unknown tongue. One of its chiefs, who understood Provencal, begged the commune of Marseilles to give them this bare and barren promontory, on which, like the sailors of the ancient times, they had run their boats ashore. The request was granted, and three months afterwards, around the twelve or fifteen small vessels which had brought these gipsies of the sea, a small village sprung up.

From Alexandre Dumas's *The Count of Monte-Cristo*

But the spectacle which most concerned the young soldier was on the western bank of the lake, though quite near to its southern termination. On a strip of land, which appeared, from his stand, too narrow to contain such an army, but which, in truth, extended many hundreds of yards from the shores of the Horican to the base of the mountain, were to be seen the white tents and military engines of an encampment of ten thousand men. Batteries were already thrown up in their front, and even while the spectators above them were looking down, with such different emotions, on a scene which lay like a map beneath their feet, the roar of artillery rose from the valley, and passed off in thundering echoes, along the eastern hills.

From James Fenimore Cooper's *The Last of the Mohicans*

Some forty minutes, Sir Ethelred, in a house of bad repute called Continental Hotel, closeted in a room which by-the-bye I took for the night. I found him under the influence of that reaction which follows the effort of crime. The man cannot be defined as a hardened criminal. It is obvious that he did not plan the death of that wretched lad his brother-in-law. That was a shock to him I could see that. Perhaps he is a man of strong sensibilities. Perhaps he was even fond of the lad who knows? He might have hoped that the fellow would get clear away; in which case it would have been almost impossible to bring this thing home to anyone. At any rate he risked consciously nothing more but arrest for him.

From Joseph Conrad's *The Secret Agent*

When opened, his gaze seemed fastened on the clouds, which hung around the western horizon, reflecting the bright colours, and giving form and loveliness to the glorious tints of an American sunset. The hour—the calm beauty of the season—the occasion, all conspired to fill the spectators with solemn awe. Suddenly, while musing on the remarkable position, in which he was placed, Middleton felt the hand, which he held, grasp his own with incredible power and the old man supported on either side by his friends rose upright to his feet. For a single moment he looked about him, as if to invite all in presence to listen... and with a voice, that might be heard in every part of that numerous assembly, he pronounced the emphatic word—"Here!"

From James Fenimore Cooper's *The Prairie: A Tale*

Seeing the hart escaped and his horse dead, he sat down by a fountain, and fell into deep thought again. And as he sat there alone, he thought he heard the noise of hounds, as it were some thirty couple in number, and looking up he saw coming towards him the strangest beast that ever he had seen or heard tell of, which ran towards the fountain and drank of the water. Its head was like a serpent's, with a leopard's body and a lion's tail, and it was footed like a stag; and the noise was in its belly, as it were the baying or questing of thirty couple of hounds. While it drank there was no noise within it; but presently, having finished, it departed with a greater sound than ever.

From Sir James Knowles's *The Legends of King Arthur and His Knights*

There was no change in the weather the following morning, the wind even blowing with greater force and the sea such as I had never seen it before, and such a sea as I hope never to experience again; so, in order that the ship might ride the more easily and those below in the engine room better able to go on with the repair of the cylinder than they could with the old barquey pitching her bows under and then kicking up her heels sky high, . . . the skipper had all our spare spars lashed together, and attaching a stout steel wire hawser to them, launched the lot overboard through a hole in the bulwarks, where one of the waves had made a convenient clean sweep, veering the hawser ahead with this "jetsam" to serve as a floating anchor for us, and moor the ship.

From John Hutcheson's *The Ghost Ship: A Mystery of the Sea*

Suddenly, however, a curious phenomenon occurred. A subtle but distinct and instantaneous change of colour took place, which made it seem as though the spectators were regarding the scene through tinted glass. All the brilliance and purity and beauty of the various hues had died out. The dazzling ultramarine of the zenith became indigo; the clear transparent hues of the horizon thickened and deepened to a leaden gray; the sun gleamed aloft pallid and rayless, like a ghost of its former self; and the ocean, black and turbid, heaved restlessly, writhing as if in torture. An intense and unnatural silence, too, seemed suddenly to have fallen upon nature, enwrapping the scene as with a mantle.

From Harry Collingwood's *The Pirate Island: A Story of the South Pacific*

"Well, Elizabeth, listen," said Lassiter. "Before you was born your father made a mortal enemy of a Mormon named Dyer. They was both ministers an' come to be rivals. Dyer stole your mother away from her home. She gave birth to you in Texas eighteen years ago. Then she was taken to Utah, from place to place, an' finally to the last border settlement—Cottonwoods. You was about three years old when you was taken away from Milly. She never knew what had become of you. But she lived a good while hopin' and prayin' to have you again. Then she gave up an' died. An' I may as well put in here your father died ten years ago. Well, I spent my time tracin' Milly, an' some months back I landed in Cottonwoods."

From Zane Grey's *Riders of the Purple Sage*

# ON THE CONTRARY

You'll find out if opposites really attract in this challenging chapter. In order to solve the following puzzles, you'll have to create a contrasting message from the content we've provided. That means that if a passage revolves around a ship setting sail on an absolutely perfect day, you'll have to conjure up a terrible storm and quickly. Some puzzles will be harder than others, so if you get stumped, just make sure the theme of each message is completely different from the story as seen in the example we've given.

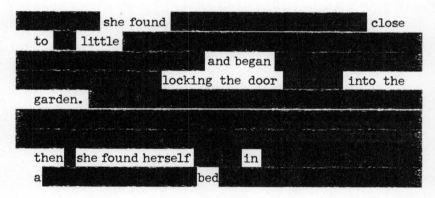

From Lewis Carroll's *Alice's Adventures in Wonderland*

**Message:** she found close to little and began locking the door into the garden./ then she found herself in a bed

He could not see what the woman was about, but heard the clish-clash of her jewellery for many minutes. A match lit up the darkness; he caught the well-known purr and fizzle of grains of incense. Then the room filled with smoke—heavy, aromatic, and stupefying. Through growing drowse he caught the names of Devils—of Zulbazan, son of Eblis, who lives in bazars and paraos, making all the sudden lewd wickedness of wayside halts; of Dulhan, invisible about mosques, the dweller among the slippers of the Faithful, who hinders folk from their prayers; and Musboot, Lord of lies and panic. Huneefa, now whispering in his ear, now talking as from an immense distance, touched him with horrible soft fingers, but Mahbub's grip never shifted from his neck till, relaxing with a sigh, the boy lost his senses.

From Rudyard Kipling's *Kim*

The man was elderly and infirm. We can understand his taking an evening stroll, but the ground was damp and the night inclement. Is it natural that he should stand for five or ten minutes, as Dr. Mortimer, with more practical sense than I should have given him credit for, deduced from the cigar ash? . . . I think it unlikely that he waited at the moor-gate every evening. On the contrary, the evidence is that he avoided the moor. That night he waited there. It was the night before he made his departure for London. The thing takes shape, Watson. It becomes coherent. Might I ask you to hand me my violin, and we will postpone all further thought upon this business until we have had the advantage of meeting Dr. Mortimer and Sir Henry Baskerville in the morning.

From Arthur Conan Doyle's *The Hound of Baskervilles*

Fortunately the cave, although not very deep, was quite dry, so that we succeeded in making ourselves much more comfortable than could have been expected. We landed our provisions, wrung the water out of our garments, spread our sail below us for a carpet, and, after having eaten a hearty meal, began to feel quite cheerful But as night drew on, our spirits sank again, for with the daylight all evidence of our security vanished away. We could no longer see the firm rock on which we lay. while we were stunned with the violence of the tempest that raged around us. The night grew pitchy dark, as it advanced, so that we could not see our hands when we held them up before our eyes, and were obliged to feel each other occasionally to make sure that we were safe.

From Robert Michael Ballantyne's *The Coral Island*

It required but very little persuasion on the part of the pirates to induce one to join them, whose spirit was congenial with theirs, so he very soon became one of the most active and daring of their number. Courage, cunning and cruelty were considered by them to be the most important qualifications of a bona-fide bucanier, and they soon found that these were possessed by Rowland, in a most superlative degree, and this added to the influence of his talents and early education, caused him to rise rapidly to a station of command among them. As it was his motto 'to make hay while the sun shines,' he sailed as soon as possible from Madagascar, from which he had not been absent but twenty days when he fell ill with and captured a Spanish Galleon, bound from Genoa to Lisbon, laden with a large amount of gold and silver ornaments, which was the property of the church, and was under the care of a number of ecclesiastics who had taken passage in this unfortunate vessel.

From Benjamin Barker's *Blackbeard; Or, the Pirate of the Roanoke*

I do not know how long I lay in that tunnel. I was roused by a soft hand touching my face. Starting up in the darkness, I snatched at my matches and hastily striking one saw three grotesque, white creatures, similar to the one I had seen above ground in the ruin, hastily retreating before the light. Living as they did in what appeared to me impenetrable darkness, their eyes were abnormally large and sensitive . . . I have no doubt they could see me in that rayless obscurity, and they did not seem to have any fear of me apart from the light. But so soon as I struck a match in order to see them, they fled incontinently, vanishing up dark gutters and tunnels from which their eyes glared at me in the strangest fashion.

From H.G. Wells's *The Time Machine*

When they arrived at Harwich they found a vessel, which had put in there, just ready to depart for Rotterdam. So they went immediately on board, and sailed with a fair wind; but they had hardly proceeded out of sight of land when a sudden and violent storm arose and drove them to the south-west; insomuch that the captain apprehended it impossible to avoid the Goodwin Sands, and he and all his crew gave themselves up for lost. Mrs Heartfree, who had no other apprehensions from death but those of leaving her dear husband and children, fell on her knees to beseech the Almighty's favour, when Wild, with a contempt of danger truly great, took a resolution as worthy to be admired perhaps as any recorded of the bravest hero, ancient or modern.

From Henry Fielding's *The History of the Life of the Late Mr. Jonathan Wild the Great*

It was now the 24th and that meant twenty days of hiding before I could venture to approach the powers that be. I reckoned that two sets of people would be looking for me—Scudder's enemies to put me out of existence, and the police, who would want me for Scudder's murder. It was going to be a giddy hunt, and it was queer how the prospect comforted me. I had been slack so long that almost any chance of activity was welcome. When I had to sit alone with that corpse and wait on Fortune I was no better than a crushed worm, but if my neck's safety was to hang on my own wits I was prepared to be cheerful about it.

From John Buchan's *The Thirty-Nine Steps*

We came to an anchor under a little island in the latitude of 23 degrees 28 minutes, being just under the northern tropic, and about twenty leagues from the island. Here we lay thirteen days, and began to be very uneasy for my friend William, for they had promised to be back again in four days, which they might very easily have done. However, at the end of thirteen days, we saw three sail coming directly to us, which a little surprised us all at first, not knowing what might be the case; and we began to put ourselves in a posture of defence; but as they came nearer us, we were soon satisfied, for the first vessel was that which William went in, carried a flag of truce.

From Daniel Defoe's *The Life, Adventures, and Piracies of the Famous Captain Singleton*

# CHAPTER NINE

# A SYLLABIC MUSING

This chapter is sure to cause a raucous! To complete these lively puzzles, you'll have to create a message using two filler words (prepositions and/or articles only!) and words with a certain number of syllables. Sure, you'll probably be able to handle one-syllabled words, but what about two- or three-syllabled words? You may find it helpful to reference the message we've created, or sound out the words if you're having a hard time figuring out the number of syllables in each word.

### Create a message using one-syllabled words.

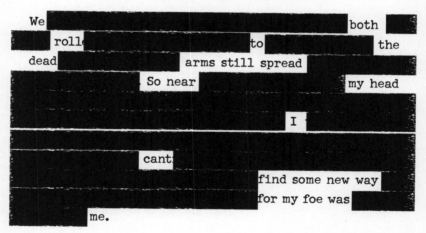

From Robert Louis Stevenson's *Treasure Island*

**Message:** We both roll to the dead/ arms still spread So near my head/ I can't find some new way for my foe was me.

**Create a message using one-syllabled words.**

While Pinocchio swam fast so as to reach the beach quickly, he perceived that his papa, who sat on his back, trembled just as if he had a high fever. Did he tremble from cold or fear? Who knows? Perhaps a little of both. But Pinocchio, believing that he trembled from fear, said to him in a comforting tone: "Courage, Papa! In a little while we shall arrive on the shore safe and sound." "But where is the shore?" asked the old man, becoming more and more uneasy and straining his eyes to see it, just as tailors do when they thread a needle. "Here we are, swimming all night; and I see only sky and sea."

From C. Collodi's *The Adventures of Pinocchio*

**Create a message using two-syllabled words.**

In truth, all through the haunted forest
there could be nothing more frightful than
the figure of Goodman Brown. On he flew
among the black pines, brandishing his staff
with frenzied gestures, now giving vent to
an inspiration of horrid blasphemy, and now
shouting forth such laughter as set all the
echoes of the forest laughing like demons
around him. The fiend in his own shape is less
hideous than when he rages in the breast of
man. Thus sped the demoniac on his course,
until, quivering among the trees, he saw a red
light before him, as when the felled trunks
and branches of a clearing have been set on
fire, and throw up their lurid blaze against
the sky, at the hour of midnight.

From Nathaniel Hawthorne's "Young Goodman Brown"

## Create a message using three-syllabled words.

We were looking over an evening edition of the "Gazette des Tribunaux," when the following paragraphs arrested our attention. "EXTRAORDINARY MURDERS. This morning, about three o'clock, the inhabitants of the Quartier St. Roch were aroused from sleep by a succession of terrific shrieks, issuing, apparently, from the fourth story of a house in the Rue Morgue, known to be in the sole occupancy of one Madame L'Espanaye, and her daughter, Mademoiselle Camille L'Espanaye. After some delay, occasioned by a fruitless attempt to procure admission in the usual manner, the gateway was broken in with a crowbar, and eight or ten of the neighbors entered, accompanied by two gendarmes. By this time the cries had ceased; but, as the party rushed up the first flight of stairs, two or more rough voices, in angry contention, were distinguished, and seemed to proceed from the upper part of the house."

From Edgar Allan Poe's "The Murders in the Rue Morgue"

**Create a message using two-syllabled words.**

Why, I must die;
And if I do not by thy hand, thou art
No servant of thy master's. Against self-
   slaughter
There is a prohibition so divine
That cravens my weak hand. Come, here's my
   heart–
Something's afore't. Soft, soft! We'll no defence!–
Obedient as the scabbard. What is here?
The scriptures of the loyal Leonatus
All turn'd to heresy? Away, away,
Corrupters of my faith! you shall no more
Be stomachers to my heart. Thus may poor fools
Believe false teachers; though those that are
   betray'd
Do feel the treason sharply, yet the traitor
Stands in worse case of woe. And thou, Posthumus,
That didst set up my disobedience 'gainst the King
My father, and make me put into contempt the suits
Of princely fellows, shalt hereafter find
It is no act of common passage but
A strain of rareness

From William Shakespeare's "Cymbeline"

159

**Create a message using one-syllabled words.**

It was, if anything, worse than in the morning, and a new and very distressing feature, vomiting, set in, and continued till dawn. Not one wink of sleep did I get that night, for I passed it in assisting Ustane, who was one of the most gentle and indefatigable nurses I ever saw, to wait upon Leo and Job. However, the air here was warm and genial without being too hot, and there were no mosquitoes to speak of. Also we were above the level of the marsh mist, which lay stretched beneath us like the dim smoke-pall over a city, lit up here and there by the wandering globes of fen fire. Thus it will be seen that we were, speaking comparatively, in clover.

From Sir Henry Rider Haggard's *She: A History of Adventure*

**Create a message using two-syllabled words.**

I encountered him frequently afterwards. At the theatre, at balls, at concerts; at the promenades in the gardens of San Georgio; at the grotesque exhibitions in the square of St. Mark; among the throng of merchants on the Exchange by the Rialto. He seemed, in fact, to seek crowds; to hunt after bustle and amusement; yet never to take any interest in either the business or gayety of the scene. Ever an air of painful thought, of wretched abstraction; and ever that strange and recurring movement, of glancing fearfully over the shoulder. I did not know at first but this might be caused by apprehension of arrest; or perhaps from dread of assassination. But, if so, why should he go thus continually abroad; why expose himself at all times and in all places?

From Washington Irving's "The Adventure of the Mysterious Stranger"

**Create a message using three-syllabled words.**

Reasoning on these assumptions, and always bearing in mind the one certain fact to guide me, that Mrs. Catherick was in possession of the Secret, I easily understood that it was Sir Percival's interest to keep her at Welmingham, because her character in that place was certain to isolate her from all communication with female neighbours, and to allow her no opportunities of talking incautiously in moments of free intercourse with inquisitive bosom friends. But what was the mystery to be concealed? Not Sir Percival's infamous connection with Mrs. Catherick's disgrace, for the neighbours were the very people who knew of it—not the suspicion that he was Anne's father, for Welmingham was the place in which that suspicion must inevitably exist. If I accepted the guilty appearances described to me as unreservedly as others had accepted them, if I drew from them the same superficial conclusion which Mr. Catherick and all his neighbours had drawn, where was the suggestion, in all that I had heard, of a dangerous secret between Sir Percival and Mrs. Catherick, which had been kept hidden from that time to this?

From Wilkie Collins's *The Woman in White*

**Create a message using two-syllabled words.**

As for Jonr island, it neither floats nor stirs, so there is no fear it should move away before you come back; the foundations of it are fixed and rooted in the profound abyss of the earth... all that I expect for advancing you to this government, is only that you wait on your master in this expedition, that there may be an end of this memorable adventure. And I here engage my honour, that whether you return on Clavileno with all the speed his swiftness promises, or that it should be your ill fortune to be obliged to foot it back like a pilgrim, begging from inn to inn, and door to door, still whenever you come you will find your island where you left it.

From Miguel de Cervantes's *The History of the Ingenious Gentleman Don Quixote of La Mancha*

# CHAPTER TEN

# ONE FOR THE BOOKS

The challenge in this chapter isn't in creating a message, but picking the *right* words. You can only use one word per line to complete each puzzle, but with over a hundred words to chose from, you'll have to make sure you pick the best ones before you put pen to paper because once you do, you'll be stuck with your choice for good. And don't even think about cheating on this one—you can only use ink!

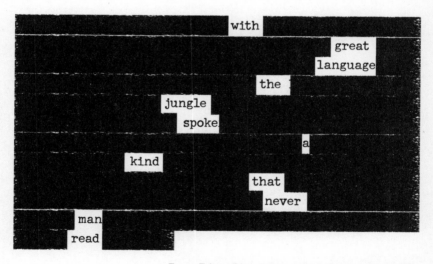

From Edgar Rice Burroughs's *Tarzan of the Apes*

**Message:** with great language the jungle spoke a kind that never man read

I set forward by a little faint track in the grass that led in my direction. It was very faint indeed to be the only way to a place of habitation; yet I saw no other. Presently it brought me to stone uprights, with an unroofed lodge beside them, and coats of arms upon the top. A main entrance it was plainly meant to be, but never finished; instead of gates of wrought iron, a pair of hurdles were tied across with a straw rope; and as there were no park walls, nor any sign of avenue, the track that I was following passed on the right hand of the pillars, and went wandering on toward the house. The nearer I got to that, the drearier it appeared. It seemed like the one wing of a house that had never been finished.

From Robert Louis Stevenson's *Kidnapped*

Gertrude had slipped out during my talk with Mrs. Watson, and I dressed and went downstairs. The billiard and card-rooms were locked until the coroner and the detectives got there, and the men from the club had gone back for more conventional clothing. I could hear Thomas in the pantry, alternately wailing for Mr. Arnold, as he called him, and citing the tokens that had precursed the murder. The house seemed to choke me, and, slipping a shawl around me, I went out on the drive. At the corner by the east wing I met Liddy . . . She had a golf-stick in her hand, and she said she had found it on the lawn. There was nothing unusual about it, but it occurred to me that a golf-stick with a metal end might have been the object that had scratched the stairs near the card-room.

From Mary Roberts Rinehart's *The Circular Staircase*

If you shut your eyes and are a lucky one, you may see at times a shapeless pool of lovely pale colours suspended in the darkness; then if you squeeze your eyes tighter, the pool begins to take shape, and the colours become so vivid that with another squeeze they must go on fire. But just before they go on fire you see the lagoon. This is the nearest you ever get to it on the mainland, just one heavenly moment; if there could be two moments you might see the surf and hear the mermaids singing. The children often spent long summer days on this lagoon, swimming or floating most of the time, playing the mermaid games in the water, and so forth.

From J.M. Barrie's *Peter and Wendy*

But when the storm had passed and the sky was clear and the mad waves had subsided into a rolling swell, there seemed no reason to believe that any one on board the "Castor" would ever reach Valparaiso. The vessel had been badly strained by the wrenching of the masts, her sides had been battered by the floating wreckage, and she was taking in water rapidly. Fortunately no one had been injured by the storm, and although the Captain found it would be a useless waste of time and labor to attempt to work the pumps, he was convinced, after a careful examination, that the ship would float some hours and that there would, therefore, be time for those on board to make an effort to save not only their lives, but some of their property.

From Frank Stockton's *The Adventures of Captain Horn*

Meanwhile the "Mongolia" was pushing forward rapidly; on the 13th, Mocha, surrounded by its ruined walls whereon date-trees were growing, was sighted, and on the mountains beyond were espied vast coffee-fields. Passepartout was ravished to behold this celebrated place, and thought that, with its circular walls and dismantled fort, it looked like an immense coffee cup and saucer. The following night they passed through the Strait of Bab-el-Mandeb, which means in Arabic "The Bridge of Tears," and the next day they put in at Steamer Point, north-west of Aden harbour, to take in coal. This matter of fueling steamers is a serious one at such distances from the coal mines; it costs the Peninsula Company some eight hundred thousand pounds a year. In these distant seas, coal is worth three or four pounds sterling a ton.

From Jules Verne's *Around the World in Eighty Days*

Ahead marched a hundred of his rovers in their short caftans of every conceivable colour, their waists swathed in gaudy scarves, some of which supported a very arsenal of assorted cutlery; many wore body armour of mail and the gleaming spike of a casque thrust up above their turbans. After them, dejected and in chains, came the five score prisoners taken aboard the Dutchman, urged along by the whips of the corsairs who flanked them. Then marched another regiment of corsairs, and after these the long line of stately, sneering camels, shuffling cumbrously along and led by shouting Saharowis. After them followed yet more corsairs, and then mounted, on a white Arab jennet, his head swathed in a turban of cloth of gold, came Sakr-el-Bahr.

From Rafael Sabatini's *The Sea Hawk*

But the Green Knight began

A low melodious laugh, like running brooks

Whose pebbly babble fills the shadowy nooks

Of green-aisled woodlands, when the winds are
    still.

"My friend, we bear each other no ill will.

When first I swung my axe, you showed some
    fear;

I owed you that much for your blow last year.

The second time I swung,—yet spared your
    life,—

That paid you for the kiss you gave my wife!"

"Your wife!" "My wife, Sir Gawain; 'twas my
    word;

And when I swung my weapon for the third

And last time, then I made the red blood spirt

For that green girdle underneath your shirt!

You played me false, my friend!"

From Jessie L. Weston's *Sir Gawain and the Green Knight*

The shore at that point was so much of a straight line as to render the hope of being able to slant-in a faint one. As it was better, however, to attempt that than to row straight in the teeth of the gale, he diverged towards a point a little to the eastward of the port of Nice, and succeeded in making better way through the water ...The gale increased. Next time he glanced over his shoulder the lights were gone. Dark clouds were gathering up from the northward, and a short jabble of sea was rising which occasionally sent a spurt of spray inboard. Feeling now that his only chance of regaining the shore lay in a strong, steady, persevering pull straight towards it, he once more turned the bow of the little boat into the wind's eye, and gave way with a will.

From Robert Michael Ballantyne's *The Madman and the Pirate*

The room was now filled with the clear light of the summer morning: the whole vision had lasted but a few seconds, but my brother knew that there was no possibility of his having been mistaken, that the mystery of the creaking chair was solved, that he had seen the man who had come evening by evening for a month past to listen to the rhythm of the *Gagliarda*. Terribly disturbed, he sat for some time half dreading and half expecting a return of the figure; but all remained unchanged; he saw nothing, nor did he dare to challenge its reappearance by playing again the *Gagliarda*, which seemed to have so strange an attraction for it.

From John Meade Falkner's *The Lost Stradivarius*

I took the bearings of a woody island that was down the river a piece, and as soon as it was fairly dark I crept out with my raft and went for it, and hid it there, and then turned in. I slept the night through, and got up before it was light, and had my breakfast, and put on my store clothes, and tied up some others and one thing or another in a bundle, and took the canoe and cleared for shore. I landed below where I judged was Phelps's place, and hid my bundle in the woods, and then filled up the canoe with water, and loaded rocks into her and sunk her where I could find her again when I wanted her, about a quarter of a mile below a little steam-sawmill that was on the bank.

From Mark Twain's *The Adventures of Huckleberry Finn*

# CHAPTER ELEVEN

# ALTERNATING TIDINGS

Like the previous chapter, you'll have to find the perfect words to complete these puzzles, but this time we made sure to kick it up a notch. Unlike before, you'll only be able to use one word from every other line to create a message, which means you'll have to pay extra attention to what you black out. While choosing words line by line is definitely much more exciting, feel free to plan ahead if you can't figure out which ones you want to get rid of.

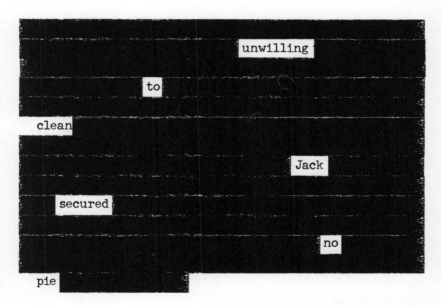

From Johann David Wyss's *The Swiss Family Robinson*

**Message:** unwilling to clean Jack secured no pie

Sir Henry and I contented ourselves with rougher arrangements, and were soon curled up in our blankets and dropping off into the dreamless sleep that rewards the traveller. Going, going, go—What was that? Suddenly from the direction of the water came a sound of violent scuffling, and next instant there broke upon our ears a succession of the most awful roars. There was no mistaking what they came from; only a lion could make such a noise as that. We all jumped up and looked towards the water, in the direction of which we saw a confused mass, yellow and black in color, staggering and struggling towards us. We seized our rifles, and, slipping on our veldtschoons (shoes made of untanned hide), ran out of the scherm towards it.

From Sir Henry Rider Haggard's *King Solomon's Mines*

I began to realise the hardihood of my expedition among these unknown people. The thicket about me became altered to my imagination. Every shadow became something more than a shadow, became an ambush; every rustle became a threat. Invisible things seemed watching me. I resolved to go back to the enclosure on the beach. I suddenly turned away and thrust myself violently, possibly even frantically, through the bushes, anxious to get a clear space about me again. I stopped just in time to prevent myself emerging upon an open space. It was a kind of glade in the forest, made by a fall; seedlings were already starting up to struggle for the vacant space... Before me, squatting together upon the fungoid ruins of a huge fallen tree and still unaware of my approach, were three grotesque human figures.

From H.G. Wells's *The Island of Doctor Moreau; a Possibility*

Aboard the rudely awakened galleon all was confused hurrying, scurrying, trumpeting, and shouting. At first there had been a desperately hurried attempt to get up the anchor; but this was abandoned as being already too late; and conceiving themselves on the point of being boarded, the Spaniards stood to arms to ward off the onslaught. Its slowness in coming intrigued them, being so different from the usual tactics of the buccaneers. Further intrigued were they by the sight of the gigantic Wolverstone speeding naked along his deck with a great flaming torch held high. Not until he had completed his work did they begin to suspect the truth—that he was lighting slow-matches—and then one of their officers rendered reckless by panic ordered a boarding-party on to the sloop, but the order came too late.

From Rafael Sabatini's *Captain Blood: His Odyssey*

It was a beautiful bright moonlight night, the sea being lighted up like a burnished mirror, and the clear orb making the distant background of the Cornish coast come out in relief, far away on our western bow. The wind being still fair for us, keeping to the east-nor'-east, Sam brought it more abeam, bearing up so that he might pass between the Wolf Rock and the Land's End, striking across the bight made by Mount's Bay in order to save the way we would have lost if he had taken the inshore track, like most coasters—and, indeed, as he would have been obliged to do if it had been foggy or rough, which, fortunately for us, it wasn't.

From John Hutcheson's *On Board the "Esmeralda" or Martin Leigh's Log*

We sons of the Achaians there sustain'd,
Both those which wand'ring on the Deep we
    bore
Wherever by Achilles led in quest
Of booty, and the many woes beside
Which under royal Priam's spacious walls
We suffer'd, know, that there our bravest fell.
There warlike Ajax lies, there Peleus' son;
There, too, Patroclus, like the Gods themselves
In council, and my son beloved there, 140
Brave, virtuous, swift of foot, and bold in
    fight,
Antilochus. Nor are these sorrows all;
What tongue of mortal man could all relate?
Should'st thou, abiding here, five years
    employ
Or six, enquiring of the woes endured
By the Achaians, ere thou should'st have
    learn'd
The whole, thou would'st depart, tir'd of the
    tale.
For we, nine years, stratagems of all kinds
Devised against them, and Saturnian Jove
Scarce crown'd the difficult attempt at last.

From Homer's *The Odyssey*

About ten men mounted the sides of the Nautilus, armed with pickaxes to break the ice around the vessel, which was soon free. The operation was quickly performed, for the fresh ice was still very thin. We all went below. The usual reservoirs were filled with the newly liberated water, and the Nautilus soon descended. I had taken my place with Conseil in the saloon: through the open window we could see the lower beds of the Southern Ocean. The thermometer went up, the needle of the compass deviated on the dial. At about 900 feet, as Captain Nemo had foreseen, we were floating beneath the undulating bottom of the iceberg. But the Nautilus went lower still—it went to the depth of four hundred fathoms.

From Jules Verne's *20,000 Leagues Under the Sea*

It was in the spring-time when they landed once more on the shores of Kn-kuul. The leaves were green and the small birds sang blithely, just as they used to do in fair Sherwood when Robin Hood roamed the woodland shades with a free heart and a light heel. All the sweetness of the time and the joyousness of everything brought back to Robin's mind his forest life, so that a great longing came upon him to behold the woodlands once more. So he went straightway to King John and besought leave of him to visit Nottingham for a short season. The King gave him leave to come and to go, but bade him not stay longer than three days at Sherwood. So Robin Hood and Allan a Dale set forth without delay to Nottinghamshire and Sherwood Forest.

From Howard Pyle's *The Merry Adventures of Robin Hood*

Kala Nag reached the crest of the ascent and stopped for a minute, and Little Toomai could see the tops of the trees lying all speckled and furry under the moonlight for miles and miles, and the blue-white mist over the river in the hollow. Toomai leaned forward and looked, and he felt that the forest was awake below him—awake and alive and crowded. A big brown fruit-eating bat brushed past his ear; a porcupine's quills rattled in the thicket, and in the darkness between the tree-stems he heard a hog-bear digging hard in the moist warm earth, and snuffing as it digged. Then the branches closed over his head again, and Kala Nag began to go down into the valley not quietly this time, but as a runaway gun goes down a steep bank in one rush.

From Rudyard Kipling's *The Jungle Book*

As we gazed a curious sound struck our ears. It seemed to begin far up in the north—a low roll like the combing of breakers on the sand. Then it grew louder and travelled nearer—a roll, with sudden spasms of harsher sound in it, reminding me of the churning in one of the pot holes of Kirkcaple cliffs. Presently it grew softer again as the sound passed south, but new notes were always emerging. The echo came sometimes, as it were, from stark rock, and sometimes from the deep gloom of the forests. I have never heard an eerier sound. Neither natural nor human it seemed, but the voice of that world between which is hid from man's sight and hearing.

John Buchan's *Prester John*

# CHAPTER TWELVE

# MORE THAN SYMBOLS

By now you may feel like you've mastered these addicting puzzles, but you haven't seen anything yet! In this final chapter, you'll need to not only create a message, but also construct it in the shape of an object. Sure, our blackout sample may make this chapter look like a piece of cake, but once you get started, you'll definitely see that this challenge is easier said than done. Just remember that you don't have to stick to a certain area of the page; anywhere and any size will do as long as you develop your message into a shape. Once you've finished, you'll have a blackout masterpiece truly worth showing off, so make sure you pass it along to friends!

**Create a message in the shape of a magnifying glass.**

It was but an hour
that the night must have almost gone, and the dawn be
breaking above us. My limbs were weary and stiff, for I
feared to change my position; yet my nerves were worked
up to the highest pitch

From Sir Arthur Conan Doyle's *Adventures of Sherlock Holmes*

**Message:** It was but an hour that the night must have almost gone, and the dawn be breaking above us./ My limbs were weary and stiff, for I feared to change my position; yet my nerves were worked up to the highest pitch

211

**Create a message in the shape of a whale.**

The four boats were soon on the water; Ahab's in advance, and all swiftly pulling toward their prey. Soon it went down, and while, with oars suspended, we were awaiting its reappearance, lo! in the same spot where it sank, once more it slowly rose. Almost forgetting for the moment all thoughts of Moby-Dick, we now gazed at the most wondrous phenomenon which the secret seas have hitherto revealed to mankind. A vast pulpy mass, furlongs in length and breadth, of a glancing cream-colour, lay floating on the water, innumerable long arms radiating from its centre, and curling and twisting like a nest of anacondas, as if blindly to clutch at any hapless object within reach.

From Herman Melville's *Moby-Dick Or, the Whale*

**Create a message in the shape of a skull.**

With his shoes on he travelled more easily, although not so swiftly, and after an hour of very rough walking he heard a sound which made him stop instantly and listen. At first he thought it might be the wind in the trees, but soon his practised ear told him that it was the sound of the surf upon the beach. Without the slightest hesitation, he made his way as quickly as possible towards the sound of the sea. In less than half an hour he found himself upon a stretch of sand which extended from the forest to the sea, and upon which the waves were throwing themselves in long, crested lines. With a cry of joy he ran out upon the beach, and with outstretched arms he welcomed the sea as if it had been an old and well-tried friend.

From Frank Stockton's *Kate Bonnet: The Romance of a Pirate's Daughter*

**Create a message in the shape of a tornado.**

In the middle of a cyclone the air is generally still, but the great pressure of the wind on every side of the house raised it up higher and higher, until it was at the very top of the cyclone; and there it remained and was carried miles and miles away as easily as you could carry a feather. It was very dark, and the wind howled horribly around her, but Dorothy found she was riding quite easily. After the first few whirls around, and one other time when the house tipped badly, she felt as if she were being rocked gently, like a baby in a cradle. Toto did not like it. He ran about the room, now here, now there, barking loudly; but Dorothy sat quite still on the floor and waited to see what would happen.

From L. Frank Baum's *The Wonderful Wizard of Oz*

**Create a message in the shape of an "X."**

My heart was beating finely when we two set
forth in the cold night upon this dangerous
venture. A full moon was beginning to rise
and peered redly through the upper edges of
the fog, and this increased our haste, for it
was plain, before we came forth again, that all
would be as bright as day, and our departure
exposed to the eyes of any watchers. We slipped
along the hedges, noiseless and swift, nor
did we see or hear anything to increase our
terrors till, to our huge relief, the door of
the "Admiral Benbow" had closed behind us.
I slipped the bolt at once, and we stood and
panted for a moment in the dark, alone in the
house with the dead captain's body.

From Robert Louis Stevenson's *Treasure Island*

**Create a message in the shape of a ship.**

They looked and rubbed their eyes to help their vision, for scarcely could they believe that which they did see. In the centre of the pale light, which extended about fifteen degrees above the horizon, there was indeed a large ship about three miles distant; but, although it was a perfect calm, she was to all appearance buffeting in a violent gale, plunging and lifting over a surface that was smooth as glass, now careening to her bearing, then recovering herself. Her topsails and mainsail were furled, and the yards pointed to the wind; she had no sail set, but a close-reefed foresail, a storm staysail, and trysail abaft. She made little way through the water, but apparently neared them fast, driven down by the force of the gale.

From Frederick Marryat's *The Phantom Ship*

**Create a message in the shape of a rabbit.**

She ran across the field after it, and was just
in time to see it pop down a large rabbit-hole
under the hedge. In another moment down
went Alice after it, never once considering
how in the world she was to get out again. The
rabbit-hole went straight on like a tunnel
for some way, and then dipped suddenly down,
so suddenly that Alice had not a moment to
think about stopping herself before she found
herself falling down what seemed to be a very
deep well. Either the well was very deep, or she
fell very slowly, for she had plenty of time as
she went down to look about her, and to wonder
what was going to happen next. First, she tried
to look down and make out what she was coming
to, but it was too dark to see anything.

From Lewis Carroll's *Alice's Adventures in Wonderland*

**Create a message in the shape of a storm cloud.**

At its setting the sun had a diminished diameter and an expiring brown, rayless glow, as if millions of centuries elapsing since the morning had brought it near its end. A dense bank of cloud became visible to the northward: it had a sinister dark olive tint, and lay low and motion-less upon the sea, resembling a solid obstacle in the path of the ship. She went floundering towards it like an exhausted creature driven to its death. The coppery twilight retired slowly, and the darkness brought out overhead a swarm of unsteady big stars that, as if blown upon, flickered exceedingly and seemed to hang very near the earth. At eight o'clock Jukes went into the chart-room to write up the ship's log.

From Joseph Conrad's *Typhoon*

**Create a message in the shape of a treasure chest.**

All that day the pirate sloop had been lying just off the shore back of the Capes, and now Tom Chist could see the sails glimmering pallidly in the moonlight, spread for drying after the storm. He was walking up the shore homeward when he became aware that at some distance ahead of him there was a ship's boat drawn up on the little narrow beach, and a group of men clustered about it. He hurried forward with a good deal of curiosity to see who had landed, but it was not until he had come close to them that he could distinguish who and what they were. Then he knew that it must be a party who had come off the pirate sloop. They had evidently just landed, and two men were lifting out a chest from the boat.

From Howard Pyle's "Tom Chist and the Treasure Box"

**Create a message in the shape of a star.**

They covered several miles before there were any signs of pursuit, and when horsemen did move into sight out of the cottonwoods Duane and his companion steadily drew farther away. "No hosses in thet bunch to worry us," called out Stevens. Duane had the same conviction, and he did not look back again. He rode somewhat to the fore, and was constantly aware of the rapid thudding of hoofs behind, as Stevens kept close to him. At sunset they reached the willow brakes and the river. Duane's horse was winded and lashed with sweat and lather. It was not until the crossing had been accomplished that Duane halted to rest his animal. Stevens was riding up the low, sandy bank. He reeled in the saddle. With an exclamation of surprise Duane leaped off and ran to the outlaw's side.

From Zane Grey's *The Lone Star Ranger*

# BIBLIOGRAPHY

Ballantyne, Robert Michael. *The Coral Island*. London: Thomas Nelson and Sons, 1884.

Ballantyne, Robert Michael. *The Madman and the Pirate*. London: Nisbet & Co., Ltd., 1883.

Barker, Benjamin. *Blackbeard; Or, the Pirate of the Roanoke*. Boston: F. Gleason, 1847.

Barrie, J.M. *Peter and Wendy*. New York: Charles Scribner's Sons, 1912.

Baum, L. Frank. *The Wonderful Wizard of Oz*. New York: G.M. Hill Co., 1900.

Bentley, E.C. *Trent's Last Case*. New York: Thomas Nelson and Sons, 1913.

Buchan, John. *Greenmantle*. New York: Hodder and Stoughton, 1916.

Buchan, John. *Prester John*. New York: Houghton Mifflin Company, 1910.

Buchan, John. *The Thirty-Nine Steps*. New York: Grosset & Dunlap, 1915.

Burroughs, Edgar Rice. *At the Earth's Core*. New York: Grosset & Dunlap, 1922.

Burroughs, Edgar Rice. *Tarzan of the Apes*. New York: A.L. Burt Company, 1914.

Carroll, Lewis. *Alice's Adventures in Wonderland*. New York: The Macmillan Company, 1898.

Carroll, Lewis. *Through the Looking Glass*. New York: Harper & Brothers, 1902.

Cervantes, Miguel de. *The History of the Ingenious Gentleman Don Quixote of La Mancha*. Trans. P. A. Motteux. Edinburgh: John Grant, 1908.

Childers, Erskine. *The Riddle of the Sands*. New York: Dodd, Mead and Company, 1915.

Collingwood, Harry. *The Pirate Island: A Story of the South Pacific*. London: Blackie and Son Limited, 1885.

Collins, Wilkie. *The Moonstone*. New York: Harper & Brothers, 1874.

Collins, Wilkie. *The Woman in White*. New York: Charles Scribner's Sons, 1908.

Collodi, C. *The Adventures of Pinocchio*. Ed. Sara E. H. Lockwood. Trans. Walter S. Cramp. Boston: Ginn and Company, 1904.

Conrad, Joseph. "Heart of Darkness." *Youth: A Narrative and Two Other Stories*. London: Willian Blackwood and Sons, 1902.

Conrad, Joseph. *The Rescue: A Romance of the Shallows*. New York: Doubleday, Page & Company, 1922.

Conrad, Joseph. *Typhoon*. New York: Doubleday, Page & Company, 1919.

Conrad, Joseph. *The Secret Agent*. Leipzig: B. Tauchnitz, 1907.

Cooper, James Fenimore. *The Last of the Mohicans*. New York: Belford, Clarke & Co., 1985.

Cooper, James Fenimore. *The Prairie: A Tale*. New York: Hurd and Houghton, 1871.

Cooper, James Fenimore. *The Spy: A Tale of the Neutral Ground*. New York: D. Appleton and Company, 1875.

Crane, Stephen. *The Red Badge of Courage*. New York: D. Appleton and Company, 1917.

Defoe, Daniel. *The Life, Adventures, and Piracies of the Famous Captain Singleton*. New York: E.P. Dutton, 1906.

Defoe, Daniel. *The Life and Adventures of Robinson Crusoe*. London: Routledge, Warne, and Routledge, 1864.

Doyle, Sir Arthur Conan. *Adventures of Sherlock Holmes*. New York: Harper & Brothers, 1902.

Doyle, Arthur Conan. *The Hound of Baskervilles*. New York: Grosset & Dunlap, 1902.

Doyle, Sir Arthur Conan. *The Lost World*. New York: Hodder & Stoughton, 1912.

Dumas, Alexandre. *The Count of Monte-Cristo*. London: Chapman and Hall, 1846.

Dumas, Alexandre. *The Three Musketeers*. Trans. William Robson. London: George Routledge and Sons, Ltd., 1922.

Falkner, John Meade. *The Lost Stradivarius*. New York: D. Appleton and Company, 1896.

Falkner, John Meade. *The Nebuly Coat*. London: Edward Arnold, 1903.

Fielding, Henry. *The History of the Life of the Late Mr. Jonathan Wild the Great*. London: J.M. Dent, Co., 1902.

Grey, Zane. *The Lone Star Ranger*. New York: Harper & Brothers, 1914.

Grey, Zane. *Riders of the Purple Sage*. New York: Harper & Brothers, 1912.

Haggard, Sir Henry Rider. *She: A History of Adventure*. London: Longmans, Green, and Co., 1887.

Haggard, Sir Henry Rider. *King Solomon's Mines*. New York: Longmans, Green and Co., 1901.

Hawthorne, Nathaniel. "Young Goodman Brown." *Mosses From an Old Manse*. Boston: Houghton, Mifflin and Company, 1893.

Henty, G.A. *The Young Buglers: A Tale of the Peninsular War*. New York: E.P. Dutton and Co., 1880.

Homer. *The Iliad of Homer*. Trans. Theodore Alois Buckley. London: William Clowes and Sons, 1873.

Homer. *The Odyssey of Homer*. Trans. George Herbert Palmer. New York: Houghton Mifflin Company, 1891.

Hope, Anthony. *The Prisoner of Zenda*. New York: Grosset & Dunlap, 1898.

Hugo, Victor. *The Hunchback of Notre-Dame*. London: Richard Bentley, 1833.

Hutcheson, John. *Crown and Anchor*. London: F.V. White & Co., 1896.

Hutcheson, John. *The Ghost Ship: A Mystery of the Sea*. London: Ward, Lock & Co., Limited, 1903.

Hutcheson, John. *On Board the "Esmeralda" or Martin Leigh's Log*. New York: Cassell and Company, Ltd., 1898.

Hutcheson, John. *Picked Up at Sea*. London: Blackie & Son, 1884.

Irving, Washington. *The Adventures of Captain Bonneville*. New York: George P. Putnam, 1850.

Irving, Washington. "The Adventure of the Mysterious Stranger." *Tales of a Traveller*. New York: C.S. Van Winkle, 1825.

Kipling, Rudyard. *Captains Courageous*. New York: Doubleday, Page & Company, 1922.

Kipling, Rudyard. *The Jungle Book*. New York: The Century Co., 1910.

Kipling, Rudyard. *Kim*. New York: Doubleday, Page & Company, 1908.

Knowles, Sir James. *The Legends of King Arthur and His Knights*. New York: Frederick Warne and Co., Ltd., 1912.

London, Jack. *The Call of the Wild*. New York: The Macmillan Company, 1920.

London, Jack. *White Fang*. New York: The Macmillan Company, 1906.

Marryat, Frederick. *The Phantom Ship*. London: Richard Bentley, 1847.

Marryat, Frederick. *The Pirate, and the Three Cutters*. Philadelphia: E.L. Carey & A. Hart, 1836.

Melville, Herman. *Moby-Dick Or, the Whale*. London: Constable and Company Ltd., 1922.

Melville, Herman. *Typee, a Romance of the South Seas*. New York: Harcourt, Brace and Company, 1920.

Mulford, Clarence. *Hopalong Cassidy*. New York: A.L. Burt Company, 1911.

Orczy, Baroness Emmuska. *The Triumph of the Scarlet Pimpernel*. New York: George H. Doran Company, 1922.

Poe, Edgar Allan. "The Murders in the Rue Morgue." *Tales*. London: Wiley & Putnam, 1846.

Poe, Edgar Allan. "The Mystery of Marie Roget." *Tales*. London: Wiley & Putnam, 1846.

Pyle, Howard. *The Merry Adventures of Robin Hood*. New York: Charles Scribner's Sons, 1883.

Pyle, Howard. "Tom Chist and the Treasure Box." *Howard Pyle's Book of Pirates*. New York: Harper & Brothers, 1921.

Rinehart, Mary Roberts. *The Circular Staircase*. New York: Grosset & Dunlap, 1908.

Rohmer, Sax. *The Insidious Dr. Fu-Manchu*. New York: Robert M. McBride & Company, 1920.

Rohmer, Sax. *The Quest of the Sacred Slipper*. New York: A.L. Burt Company, 1914.

Rohmer, Sax. *Tales of Secret Egypt*. New York: Robert M. McBride & Company, 1920.

Sabatini, Rafael. *Captain Blood: His Odyssey*. New York: Grosset & Dunlap, 1922.

Sabatini, Rafael. *Scaramouche: A Romance of the French Revolution*. Boston: Houghton Mifflin Company, 1921.

Sabatini, Rafeal. *The Sea Hawk*. Toronto: Thomas Allen, 1915.

Scott, Sir Walter. *Ivanhoe*. New York: D. Appleton and Company, 1904.

Shakespeare, William. "Cymbeline." *The Works of Shakespeare*. Ed. Edward Dowden. London: Methuen and Co., 1903.

Shakespeare, William. "The Tempest." *Shakespeare: Selected Plays*. Ed. William Aldis Wright. London: Macmillan and Co., 1875.

Stevenson, Robert Louis. *Kidnapped*. New York: Harper & Brothers, 1921.

Stevenson, Robert Louis. *The Master of Ballantrae: A Winter's Tale*. New York: F.M. Lupton, 1890.

Stevenson, Robert Louis. *Treasure Island*. New York: Harper & Brothers, 1915.

Stockton, Frank. *The Adventures of Captain Horn*. New York: Charles Scribner's Sons, 1906.

Stockton, Frank. *Kate Bonnet: The Romance of a Pirate's Daughter*. New York: D. Appleton and Company, 1902.

Stockton, Frank. "Prince Hassak's March." *The Novels and Stories of Frank R. Stockton*. New York: Charles Scribner's Sons, 1900.

Swift, Jonathan. *Gulliver's Travels into Several Remote Nations of the World*. London: The Temple Press, 1889.

Twain, Mark. *The Adventures of Tom Sawyer*. Hartford: The American Publishing Company, 1876.

Twain, Mark. *The Adventures of Huckleberry Finn*. New York: Harper & Brothers, 1899.

Twain, Mark. *A Connecticut Yankee in King Arthur's Court*. New York: Harper & Brothers, 1917.

Verne, Jules. *20,000 Leagues Under the Sea*. New York: George Munro's Sons, 1883.

Verne, Jules. *Around the World in Eighty Days*. Boston: James R. Osgood and Company, 1873.

Verne, Jules. *A Journey to the Centre of the Earth*. New York: Charles Scribner's Sons, 1905.

Verne, Jules. *The Mysterious Island*. London: Sampson Low, Marston, Low, & Searle, 1875.

Wallace, Edgar. *The Four Just Men*. Boston: Small, Maynard & Company, 1920.

Wells, H.G. *The Island of Doctor Moreau; a Possibility*. New York: Stone & Kimball, 1896.

Wells, H.G. *The Time Machine*. New York: Henry Holt and Company, 1895.

Wells, H.G. *The War of the Worlds*. London: William Heinemann, 1898.

Weston, Jessie L., Ed. *Sir Gawain and the Green Knight*. London: David Nutt, 1898.

Wiggin, Kate Douglas and Nora Smith, Ed. "The Story of Aladdin; or, the Wonderful Lamp." *The Arabian Nights*. New York: Charles Scribner's Sons, 1909.

Wiggin, Kate Douglas and Nora Smith, Ed. "The Story of Sinbad the Voyager." *The Arabian Nights*. New York: Charles Scribner's Sons, 1909.

Wister, Owen. *The Virginian; A Horseman of the Plains*. New York: The Macmillan Company, 1904.

Wyatt, Alfred John, Ed. *Beowulf*. New York: The Macmillan Company, 1901.

Wyss, Johann David. *The Swiss Family Robinson*. New York: Macmillian & Co. Limited, 1907.